THE SEASONS

Fall

D1530911

BARRON'S

Vacations are over and
the weather is
cooler.
Guess which
season it is.

There are four seasons:
winter, spring, summer,
and . . .
do you know
the last one?

3

When fall arrives,
the world wears
all kinds of colors.
You know all these
colors,
don't you?

4

How about picking up leaves from the ground and making a picture with them?

Going back to school is fun and so is singing songs about the new season and going to the woods looking for *chestnuts*.

And having Fall parties!

In the fall, many trees drop their leaves and they are naked, without a single leaf! And the ground is full of *mushrooms.* Can you see how many there are?

It often rains a lot in the fall. It is time to go outside wearing a raincoat, carrying an umbrella, and wearing boots to step into puddles.

Let's keep the *snails* company !

It is often *windy* too. The wind sweeps the fallen leaves from the ground and messes your hair. It is a perfect time to fly a kite!

It gets colder, it rains, it is windy, and you go back to *school*. Look at all these drawings. What things do you relate to fall?

15

Swallows don't like cold weather; that's why they fly away before winter comes. They take a very long trip, flying over woods, towns, rivers, and seas. Can you imagine that?

Not all animals go away when the cold weather comes. Some, such as ants, finish stocking their pantry. How many *ants* can you count? If you look carefully, you will discover where they lay their eggs.

The sun sets earlier every day. The afternoon is not as long as in summer and it gets colder and colder at *night.* It is time to go to bed early. What time do you usually go to bed?

See how many *fruits* there are at the market: apples, walnuts, . . . They are all fall fruits and many animals keep them in

their lairs or dens for the wintertime.
From the previous page, do you
know which ones are kept?

If you walk in the woods you can pick *blackberries* and make marmalade or with the fruits at the market you can make compotes and pies. Mmmmmm! It smells good!

24

When *harvest* time is over,
the farmers plow the land for winter.
The fields will then be ready for
sowing when spring comes.

How about singing a *song*?
Ask your parents if they know one,
sing with them, and then think:
what do you like best from the fall?

Let's make a compote

For this activity you will need the help of an adult. Shall we start? You will need the following ingredients: one orange, two apples, and a handful of raisins (approximately half an ounce).

apple

orange

seeds

tablespoon

colander

teaspoon

knife

juicer

pot

plate

bowl

1. Squeeze the juice out of the orange.
2. Pare both apples, take out the core and seeds, and cut the apples in round slices.
3. Place all the round slices in a cooking pan; add three tablespoons of orange juice and the raisins.
4. Put the pan over medium heat for about fifteen minutes.
5. Finally, pass everything through a colander.
6. And . . . it is ready! Try it with a cookie.

It will be delicious!

A paper bird

Have you seen swallows flying? Very often they keep still in the air, without flapping their wings. When they do that, we say they are gliding. You can see how they do it if you make your own paper bird. Do you want to try?

• Take a regular sheet of paper and follow the illustrated instructions.

Now you have a gliding bird. Does it go far? You can compete against your friends. Use a piece of chalk to mark the place where it lands.

The bird that flies the farthest wins!

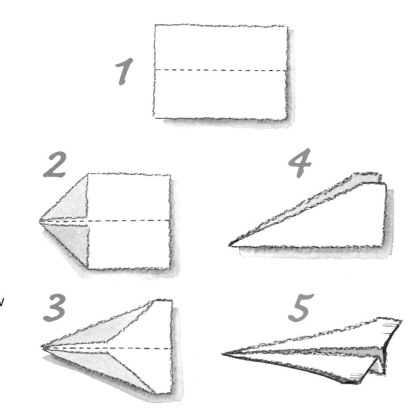

Let's make a bat

Bats can fly, but did you know they are not birds? They look more like mice, only with wings. Shall we make one?

1. Put two plastic glasses mouth to mouth and glue them together.
2. Paint them with black tempera paint.
3. Combine some pieces of white and black cardboard to make two eyes and two pointed ears. Glue them to the upper part.
4. Paint a mouth on the front and add a couple of fangs.
5. Get some more black cardboard and cut out the wings.
6. Now glue them to the sides.

It isn't scary, is it?

Guide for the parents

The months of the year

Fall begins at the end of September, it goes through October and November, and finishes at the end of December. In other words, fall is from September 21st to December 21st. You can explain this to the children as you show it on a calendar. According to the children's ages, you can review all the months of the year.

The hours

In the fall, it gets darker earlier. This chapter may be useful to check what time the children go to bed, if it has been dark for a short or a long time, where the sun is when they leave school, or when they have supper, etc. According to the children's ages, you may teach them to tell time. With the smaller children we can play to recognize the numbers up to 12, what time they get up, what time they go to bed . . . With older children we can use the opportunity to teach them about hours and minutes. If they already know that, we might practice with activities in which hours play a key role.

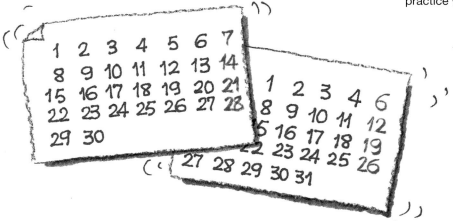

Squirrels store up food

In the illustration of fall fruits you can find a lot of dried fruits; these are the fruits some animals store up for winter use, since they stay edible for a long time.

Bird migration

When it starts getting cold, many animals migrate to warmer areas to spend the winter, for example the swallows and the storks. We call them migratory birds and you can see them all during the fall flying in formation. Other animals, such as squirrels and ants, work hard in the fall to stock their dens for winter, as there is not much food available then.

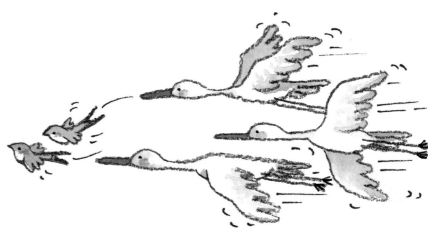

Fall festivities and songs

The beginning of a season is a good time to mark up all the festivities of the period with the children and think about celebrations: special pies and cakes, decorations for the house or for the kids themselves. They usually do all this at school, so it is just a question of posting the drawings they bring home and singing along the songs they have learned. And if you know more songs or want to decorate your home, you will no doubt have the children's help!

Original book title in Catalan: *La Tardor*
© Copyright Gemser Publications S.L., 2004.
C/Castell, 38; Teià (08329) Barcelona, Spain (World Rights)
Tel: 93 540 13 53
E-mail: *info@mercedesros.com*
Author: Núria Roca
Illustrator: Rosa Maria Curto

First edition for the United States and Canada (exclusive
rights), and the rest of the world (non-exclusive rights)
published in 2004 by Barron's Educational Series, Inc.

Address all inquiries to:
Barron's Educational Series, Inc.
250 Wireless Boulevard
Hauppauge, New York 11788
http://www.barronseduc.com

ISBN-13: 978-0-7641-2729-8
ISBN-10: 0-7641-2729-2
Library of Congress Catalog Card Number 2004101356

Printed in China
9 8

THE SEASONS

Fall